T0083345

# Alan Bullard

# O Come, Emmanuel

An Advent Celebration based on the Great 'O' Antiphons

for SATB choir and organ or piano
with optional soloists, congregation, and small orchestra or chamber group

MUSIC DEPARTMENT

OXFORD
UNIVERSITY PRESS

# Instrumentation

The work may be accompanied in two ways:

1. With **organ or piano**, using the accompaniment printed in the vocal score. Pianists may omit the small notes.

2. With **small orchestra** or **chamber group**, as follows: 1 Flute, 1 Oboe, 1 Clarinet in A, 1 Bassoon (or Bass Clarinet), 1 Trumpet in B flat, 1 Horn in F, together with *either* string quintet (2 violins, viola, cello, double bass), *or* string orchestra, *or* keyboard (piano or organ). The keyboard part here is an alternative to the string parts, and not the same as the accompaniment printed in the vocal score. The full score and set of parts are available to hire from the publisher's Hire Library or appropriate agent.

OXFORD
UNIVERSITY PRESS

Great Clarendon Street, Oxford OX2 6DP,
United Kingdom

Oxford University Press is a department of the University of Oxford.
It furthers the University's aim of excellence in research, scholarship,
and education by publishing worldwide. Oxford is a registered trade mark of
Oxford University Press in the UK and in certain other countries

© Oxford University Press 2013

Alan Bullard has asserted his right under the Copyright, Designs
and Patents Act, 1988, to be identified as the Composer of this Work

First published 2013

Impression: 6

All rights reserved. No part of this publication may be reproduced,
stored in a retrieval system, or transmitted, in any form or by any means,
without the prior permission in writing of Oxford University Press,
or as expressly permitted by law.

Permission to perform this work in public (except in the course of divine worship)
should normally be obtained from a local performing right licensing organization,
unless the owner or the occupier of the premises being used already holds a licence
from such an organization. Likewise, permission to make and exploit a recording of this work
should be obtained from a local mechanical copyright licensing organization

Enquiries concerning reproduction outside the scope of the above
should be directed to the Music Rights Department, Oxford University Press,
at music.permissions.uk@oup.com or at the address above

ISBN 978-0-19-339765-1

Printed in Great Britain on acid-free paper by
Halstan & Co. Ltd., Amersham, Bucks.

# Contents


| | | |
|---|---|---|
| | Text | 4 |
| 1. | Prelude | 10 |
| 2. | Advent Responsory (i) | 11 |
| 3. | Hymn: The advent of our God | 13 |
| 4. | O Wisdom \| O Sapientia | 15 |
| 5. | Where shall Wisdom be found? | 15 |
| 6. | O Lord of Lords \| O Adonaï | 18 |
| 7. | Come, thou long-expected Jesus | 18 |
| 8. | O Root of Jesse \| O Radix Jesse | 23 |
| 9. | There is a rose-tree | 23 |
| 10. | O Key of David \| O Clavis David | 25 |
| 11. | Earth grown old | 25 |
| 12. | Hymn: Thy kingdom come! on bended knee | 29 |
| 13. | O Morning Star \| O Oriens | 31 |
| 14. | Chanticleer | 32 |
| 15. | O King of the Nations \| O Rex Gentium | 38 |
| 16. | Hymn: Joy to the world! | 39 |
| 17. | And they shall call his name Emmanuel | 43 |
| 18. | O Emmanuel | 43 |
| 19. | Gabriel's Message | 44 |
| 20. | And art thou come with us to dwell? | 49 |
| 21. | Advent Responsory (ii) | 53 |
| 22. | Hymn: Lo! he comes with clouds descending | 55 |


# Composer's note

*O Come, Emmanuel* is designed for liturgical use or as a concert piece. If performed liturgically, the congregation can join in the four hymns as marked. Optional Bible readings are suggested—they may not all be used, or they may be replaced with others. If performed in a concert situation—probably without readings—the hymns (sung by the choir) can be shortened or omitted as shown.

The work is designed with some flexibility in mind, and may be sung entirely by SATB choir, with groups of singers (or the whole choir) taking the unison lines as indicated, or by SATB choir with a range of soloists. Many of the movements, including the settings of 'There is a rose-tree' and 'Chanticleer' may be performed separately during the Advent / Christmas season.

The work could be used for a 'darkness to light' service. The choir could sing the first Advent Responsory from the back, and move forward to intermediate positions during the first two hymns, reaching the front during 'Joy to the World'.

Duration without readings: *c.*35 minutes.

# Text

The fundamental text is drawn from the seven Great 'O' Antiphons, paraphrased from the original Latin. These passages, traditionally used in church services in the final days of Advent, are here combined with musical phrases from Advent hymns, notably 'O come, O come Emmanuel' (the text of which is itself based on these same antiphons). The other movements are all related in some way to these sections, either textually or musically, and consist of a range of original material together with arrangements of familiar Advent hymns or carols.

**1. Prelude**

(optional words)
O come, O come, Emmanuel,
And ransom captive Israel,
That mourns in lonely exile here,
Until the Son of God appear:
Rejoice! Rejoice! Emmanuel
Shall come to thee, O Israel.

Latin trad., tr. J. M. Neale

**2. Choir: Advent Responsory (i)**

I look from afar: and lo I see the power of God coming, and a cloud covering the whole earth. Go ye out to meet him, and say: Tell us, tell us, art thou He that should come to reign over thy people Israel?

The Matin Responsory

**3. Hymn: The advent of our God**

1. The advent of our God
With eager hearts we greet,
And, singing, haste upon the road
His coming reign to meet.

3. Daughter of Sion, rise
To meet thy lowly king;
Let not thy heart in haste despise
The peace he comes to bring.

3. All glory to the Son
Who comes to set us free,
With Father, Spirit, ever one,
Through all eternity.

2. For, lo, God's word and Son
Came down to make us free,
And he a servant's form put on,
To bring us liberty.

4. As judge, on clouds of light,
He soon will come again,
And all his scatter'd saints unite
With him in heav'n to reign.

C. Coffin
vv. 1–3 tr. Percy Dearmer
vv. 4–5 tr. John Chandler

**4. O Wisdom | O Sapientia**

O Wisdom, which comes from the mouth of the Most High, and reaches to the ends of the earth: Show us the way of knowledge.

Great 'O' Antiphon No. 1, paraphrased AB

**5. Choir: Where shall Wisdom be found?**

But where shall wisdom be found? And where is the place of understanding? Behold, the love* of the Lord: that is wisdom. And to depart from evil is understanding.

* or *fear* (as in Authorized Version)

Job 28: 12 and 28

**6. O Lord of Lords | O Adonaï**

O Lord of Lords and ruler of Israel, who appeared to Moses in the flame of the burning bush, and who gave to him the law on Sinai: Come and redeem us with outstretched arm.

Great 'O' Antiphon No. 2, paraphrased AB

**7. Choir: Come, thou long-expected Jesus**

Come, thou long-expected Jesus,
Born to set thy people free,
From our fears and sins release us,
Let us find our rest in Thee.
Israel's strength and consolation,
Hope of all the earth thou art;
Dear desire of ev'ry nation,
Joy of ev'ry longing heart.

Born thy people to deliver,
Born a child and yet a king,
Born to reign in us for ever,
Now thy gracious kingdom bring.
By thine own eternal Spirit
Rule in all our hearts alone;
By thine all-sufficient merit
Raise us to thy glorious throne.

Come, thou long-expected Jesus,
Come, Lord Jesus, come!

Charles Wesley

**8. O Root of Jesse | O Radix Jesse**

O root of Jesse, who stands as a sign to the people, silencing kings and interceding for nations: Come and save us without delay.

Great 'O' Antiphon No. 3, paraphrased AB

**9. Choir: There is a rose-tree**

1. There is a rose-tree blooming
In winter's frost and cold;
Its flower comes from Jesse,
A sign of peace from old.
It is the Rose of Love,
No cruel wind can wither,
No tempest can remove.

2. It was Isaiah who told us:
This rose of which we sing
Brings us the Virgin Mary,
The mother of our King.
It is the Rose of Love,
No cruel wind can wither,
No tempest can remove.

3. Lo, any life that shivers
May shelter 'neath that tree,
Each tender petal quivers
With glowing mystery.
Amid the sweetness curled
A golden heart is hidden,
The future of the world!

Es ist ein Ros entsprungen, tr. Abbie Farwell Brown, altd.

**10. O Key of David | O Clavis David**

O Key of David, and Sceptre of the House of Israel, you open and none can close, you close and none can open: Come and release the captives from the shadow of darkness.

Great 'O' Antiphon No. 4, paraphrased AB

**11. Choir: Earth grown old**

1. Earth grown old, yet still so green,
And deep beneath her crust of cold
Hidden fire, unfelt, unseen:
Earth grown old.

2. The race that long in darkness pined
Have seen a glorious light:
The people dwell in day, who dwelt
In death's surrounding night.

3. When will fire break through her screen?
And when will life burst through her mould?
Earth, reborn, thy light is seen:
Silver, gold.

4. A Child of Hope to us is born,
A Son to us is giv'n:
The tribes of earth obey his word,
Likewise the hosts of heav'n.

5. Welcome, all wonders in one sight!
Eternity shut in a span!
Summer in winter, day in night,
God in man!

6. The Prince of Peace shall be his name,
For evermore adored;
The Wonderful, the Counsellor,
The great and mighty Lord.

vv. 1 and 3: Christina Rossetti
v. 5: Richard Crashaw
vv: 2, 4, and 6: Isaiah 9: 2, 6, paraphrased John Morison, altd.

**12: Hymn: Thy kingdom come! on bended knee**

1. Thy kingdom come! on bended knee
The passing ages pray;
And faithful souls have yearned to see
On earth that kingdom's day.

2. But the slow watches of the night
Not less to God belong;
And for the everlasting right
The silent stars are strong.

3. And lo, already on the hills
The flags of dawn appear;
Gird up your loins, ye prophet souls,
Proclaim the day is near:

4. The day in whose clear-shining light
All wrong shall stand revealed,
When justice shall be throned in might,
And ev'ry hurt be healed;

5. When knowledge, hand in hand with peace,
Shall walk the earth abroad:
The day of perfect righteousness,
The promised day of God.

F. L. Hosmer

**13. O Morning Star | O Oriens**

O Morning Star, the brightness of eternal light and justice: Come and illuminate those who live in darkness and the shadow of death.

Great 'O' Antiphon No. 5, paraphrased AB

**14. Choir: Chanticleer**

All this night shrill chanticleer*,
Day's proclaiming trumpeter,
Claps his wings and loudly cries,
Mortals, mortals, wake and rise!
See a wonder
Heav'n is under;
From the earth is ris'n a Sun,
Shines all night, though day be done.

Wake, O earth, wake ev'rything!
Wake, and hear the joy I bring:
Wake and joy; for all this night
Heaven and ev'ry twinkling light,
All amazing,
Still stand gazing,
Angels, Powers and all that be,
Wake and joy this Sun to see.

Hail, O Sun, O blessed Light,
Sent into the world by night!
Let thy rays and heav'nly powers
Shine in these dark souls of ours;
For most duly
Thou art truly
God and man, we do confess:
Hail, O Sun of righteousness!

* chanticleer = a crowing cockerel

William Austin

**15. O King of the Nations | O Rex Gentium**

O King of all the nations, the cornerstone which binds all peoples together: Come and save humanity which you have made out of clay.

Great 'O' Antiphon No. 6, paraphrased AB

**16. Hymn: Joy to the world!**

1. Joy to the world! the Lord is come;
   Let earth receive her King;
   Let ev'ry heart prepare him room,
   And heav'n and nature sing.

2. Joy to the world! the Saviour reigns;
   Let all their songs employ;
   While fields and flocks, rocks, hills and plains
   Repeat the sounding joy.

3. No more let thorns infest the ground,
   Or sins and sorrows grow.
   Wherever troubles and cares are found
   He makes his blessings flow.

4. He rules the world with truth and grace,
   And makes the nations prove
   The glories of his righteousness
   And wonders of his love.

Paraphrase of Psalm 98 by Isaac Watts, altd.

**17. And they shall call his name Emmanuel**

And they shall call his name Emmanuel, which being interpreted is God with us.

Matthew 1: 23

**18. O Emmanuel**

O Emmanuel, our king and lawgiver, the hope and the saviour of all the nations: Come and save us, O Lord our God.

Great 'O' Antiphon No. 7, paraphrased AB

**19. Choir: Gabriel's Message**

1. The Angel Gabriel from heaven came,
   His wings as drifted snow, his eyes as flame;
   'All hail,' said he, 'thou lowly maiden Mary,
   Most highly favoured lady'. Gloria!

2. 'For known a blessed mother thou shalt be,
   All generations laud and honour thee,
   Thy son shall be Emmanuel, by seers foretold.
   Most highly favoured lady'. Gloria!

3. Then gentle Mary meekly bowed her head,
   'To me be as it pleaseth God,' she said.
   'My soul shall laud and magnify his holy name':
   Most highly favoured lady. Gloria!

4. Of her, Emmanuel the Christ was born
   In Bethlehem, all on a Christmas morn,
   And Christian folk throughout the world will ever say:
   'Most highly favoured lady'. Gloria!

Trad. text, paraphrased S. Baring-Gould

**20. Choir: And art thou come with us to dwell?**

1. And art thou come with us to dwell,
   Our prince, our guide, our love, our Lord?
   And is thy name Emmanuel,
   God present with his world restored?

2. [ The heart is glad for thee: it knows
   No-one shall bid it err or mourn,
   And o'er its desert breaks the rose
   In triumph o'er the grieving thorn.

   O come, o come, Emmanuel, And ransom captive Israel. ]

3. Thou bringest all again; with thee
   Is light, is space, is breadth, and room
   For each thing fair, beloved and free,
   To have its hour of life and bloom.

4. [ Each deepest instinct, unconfessed;
   Each hidden root, each cloud above,
   And all that life hath long repressed,
   Unfolds, revealing joy and love.

   That mourns in lonely exile here, Until the Son of God appear. ]

5. Thy reign eternal will not cease;
   Thy years are sure and glad, and strong,
   Within thy glorious world of peace
   The humblest creature makes its song.

6. The world is glad for thee: the heart
Is glad for thee, and all is well
And fixed, and sure, because thou art,
Whose name is called Emmanuel.

Rejoice, rejoice, Emmanuel Shall come to thee, O Israel.

Dora Greenwell, altd.
Latin trad., tr. J. M. Neale

**21. Advent Responsory (ii)**

Judah and Jerusalem, fear not, nor be dismayed; Tomorrow go ye forth, and the Lord he will be with you. Stand ye still, and ye shall see the salvation of the Lord. Glory be to the Father, and to the Son, and to the Holy Ghost.

The Vesper Responsory

**22. Hymn: Lo! He comes with clouds descending**

1. Lo! he comes with clouds descending,
Once for favoured sinners slain:
Thousand, thousand saints attending,
Swell the triumph of his train:
Alleluia! Alleluia!
God appears on earth to reign.

2. Ev'ry eye shall now behold him
Robed in awesome majesty:
We, who set at nought and sold him,
Crucified him on the tree,
Lord, have mercy, Lord, have mercy,
Let us all thine Advent see!

3. Those dear tokens of his passion
Still his dazzling body bears:
Cause of endless exultation
To his ransomed worshippers,
Sing hosanna, Sing hosanna,
See, the risen Lord appears!

4. Yea, Amen! let all adore thee,
High on thine eternal throne;
Saviour, take the pow'r and glory:
Claim the kingdom for thine own;
O come quickly! O come quickly!
Alleluia! Come, Lord, come!

Charles Wesley, altd.

*for Sarah MacDonald and the Chapel Choir of Selwyn College, Cambridge*

# O Come, Emmanuel

## An Advent Celebration based on the Great 'O' Antiphons

**ALAN BULLARD**

## 1. Prelude

Latin trad., tr. J. M. Neale (1818–66)

VENI EMMANUEL
(Anon. 15th century)

* The Prelude may **either** be played on solo organ (not piano) sounding as if in the distance, **or** sung by two or four solo sopranos or altos, using the words printed in brackets. The solo singers could be off-stage, or placed antiphonally around the performance space, moving back to the choir before or during the second movement.

This work may be accompanied either by organ or piano alone (using this score), or by small orchestra or chamber group, as follows: 1 Fl., 1 Ob., 1 Cl. in A, 1 Bn.(or B.Cl.), 1 Tpt. in B flat, 1 Hn. in F, together with **either** string quintet, **or** string orchestra, **or** keyboard (piano or organ). The full score and set of parts (including keyboard) are available on hire from the Publisher's Hire Library.

© Oxford University Press 2013

Printed in Great Britain

OXFORD UNIVERSITY PRESS, MUSIC DEPARTMENT, GREAT CLARENDON STREET, OXFORD OX2 6DP
The Moral Rights of the Composer have been asserted. Photocopying this copyright material is ILLEGAL.

# 2. Choir: Advent Responsory (i)

The Matin Responsory

Alan Bullard, based on HELMSLEY
Martin Madan (1726–90)

Freely
TUTTI or SOLO
a tempo ♩ = c.104
25
f as before
Go ye out to meet him, and say:
mf
29
mf brightly
S.
A.
Tell us, tell us, art thou He that should
TUTTI
Tell us, tell us,
T.
B.
mf brightly
f
33
poco rit.
come to reign ov - er thy peo - ple Is - ra - el?
p
poco rit.
p

# 3. Hymn: The advent of our God

C. Coffin (1676–1749)
vv. 1–3 tr. Percy Dearmer (1867–1936)
and vv. 4–5 tr. John Chandler (1806–76)

ST THOMAS
William's Psalmody, 1770
vv. 2, 4 and 5 arr. Alan Bullard

*Verses 3 and 4 may be omitted

53
f
free, And he a ser - vant's form put on, To bring us li - ber - ty.
- gain, And all his scat - ter'd saints u - nite With him in heav'n to reign.
f
f
SOPRANO DESCANT
58
f
S.
5. All glo - ry to the Son Who comes to set us free, With
ALL OTHER VOICES
f
A.
T.
B.
5. All glo - ry to the Son Who comes to set us free, With
f
f
62
rit.
Fa - ther, Spi - rit, ev - er one, Through all e - ter - ni - ty.
Fa - ther, Spi - rit, ev - er one, Through all e - ter - ni - ty.
rit.

Optional READING: Ecclesiasticus 24: 1–9 (or Job 28: 12–13, 23–28)

# 4. O Wisdom | O Sapientia

Great 'O' Antiphon No. 1, paraphrased AB

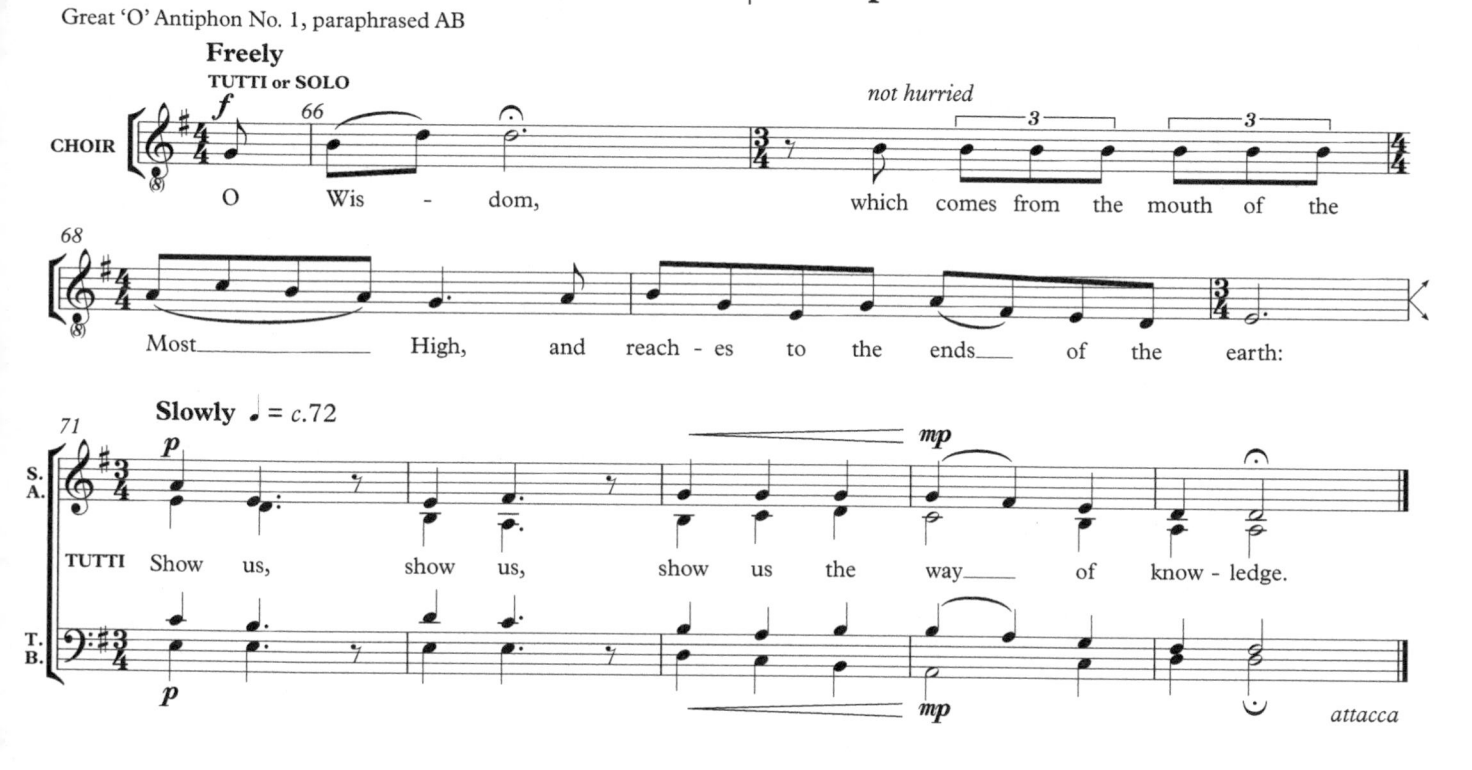


# 5. Choir: Where shall Wisdom be found?

Job 28: 12 and 28

Alan Bullard

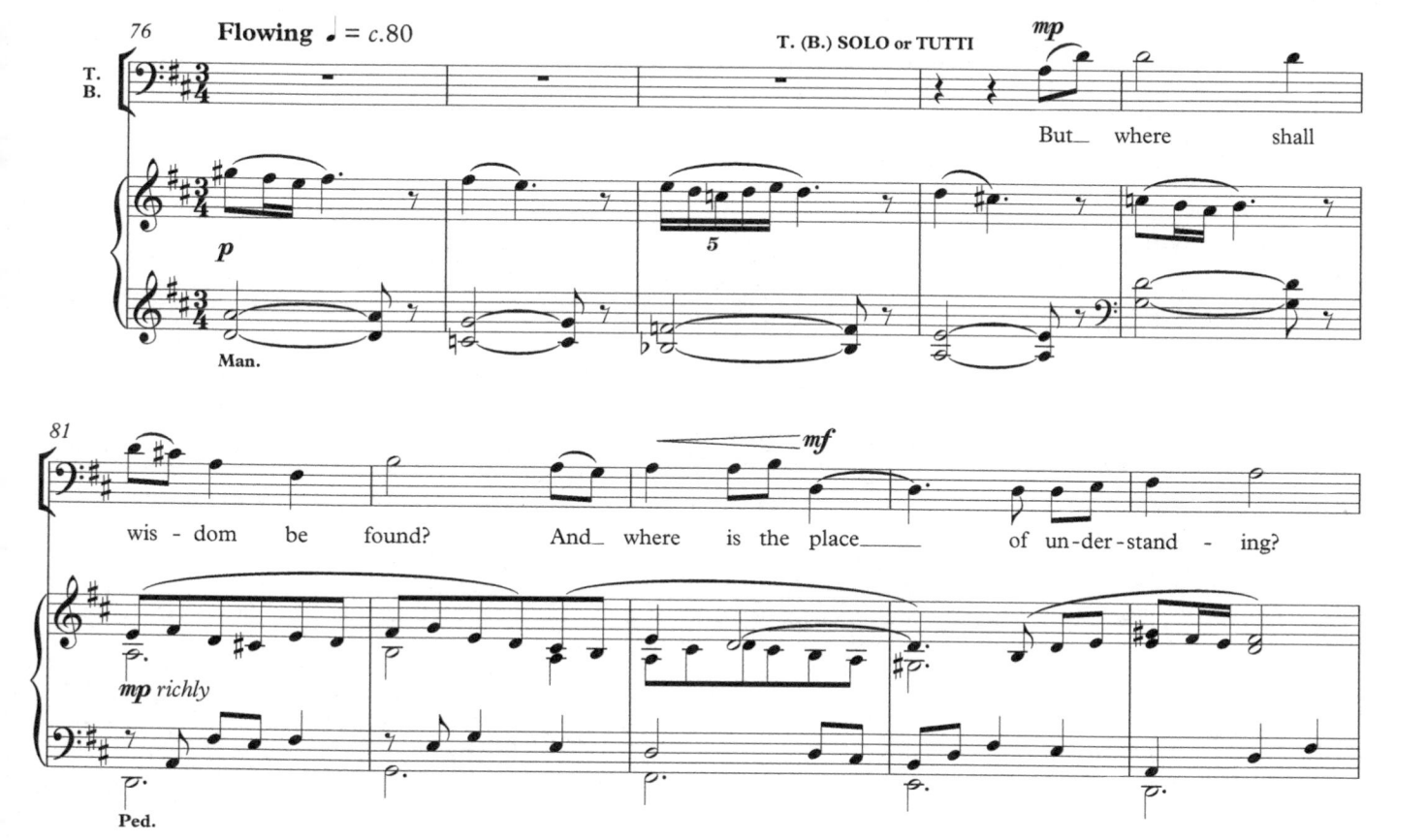

* or *fear* (as in Authorized Version)

103
tenuto
p
mp
a tempo
Lord: that is wis - dom, wis - dom.
Lord: that is wis - dom,
tenuto
p
a tempo
mp
Man.
109
A little slower
p
molto rit.
And to de-part from e - vil is un - der-
p
A little slower
molto rit.
114
a tempo
mf
rit.
p
- stand - - - - - ing, un-der-stand - ing.
- stand - - - - - - ing, un-der - stand - ing.
mf
p
un-der-stand - ing.
a tempo
rit.
mp richly
p
pp
Ped.

Optional READING: Exodus 3: 1–6

# 6. O Lord of Lords | O Adonaï

Great 'O' Antiphon No. 2, paraphrased AB

# 7. Choir: Come, thou long-expected Jesus

Charles Wesley (1707–88)

Alan Bullard

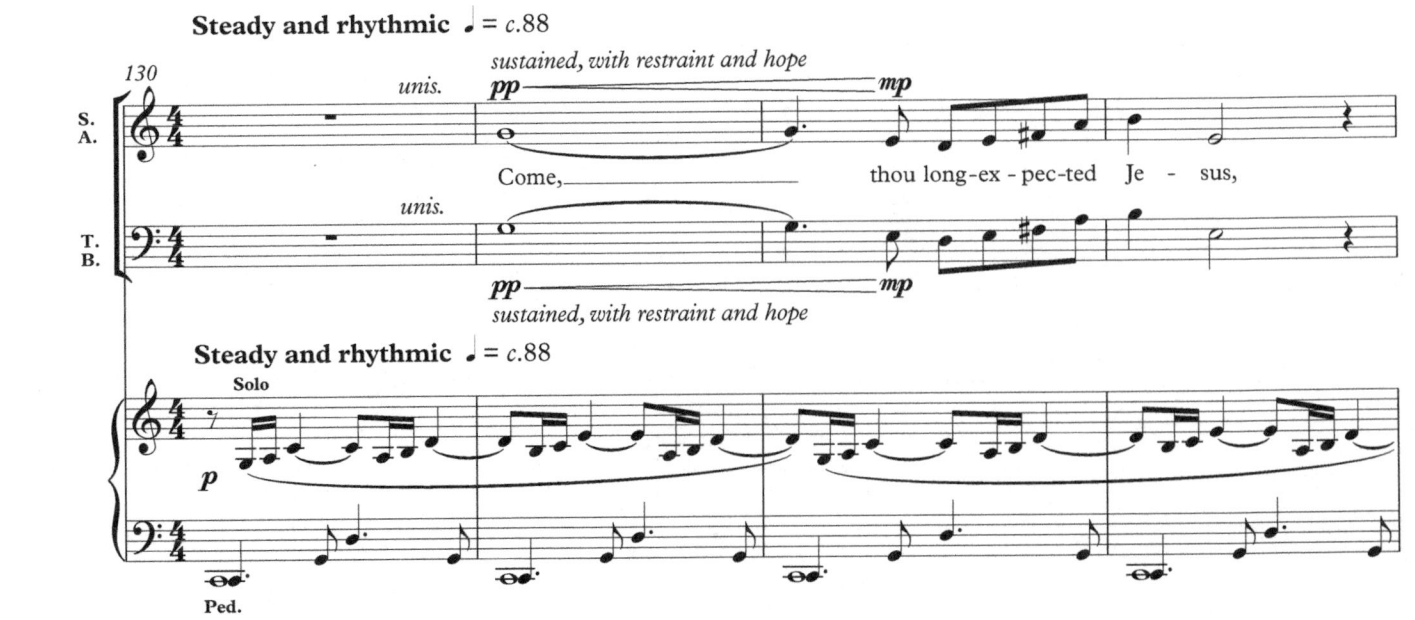

134
mf
f
Born to set thy peo-ple free, From our fears and sins re-lease us,
mf
f
f
138
p
mf
Let us find our rest in Thee.
p
mf
p
142
p legato ed espress.
mp
Is - rael's strength and con - so - la - tion, Hope of all the
p legato ed espress.
mp
p

146
f
earth thou art; Dear de - sire of ev - 'ry na - tion, Joy of ev - 'ry
f
f
150
more positive
fp
long - - ing heart. Born
fp
more positive
p
154
mf
f
thy peo-ple to de - liv - er, Born a child and yet a king,
mf
f

158
Born to reign in us for ev - er, Now thy gra - cious king - dom
p
f
p
162
mf
bring.
f joyfully but still sustained
By thine own e - ter - nal Spi - rit Rule in all our
mf
f joyfully but still sustained
f
167
hearts a - lone; By thine all - suf - fi - cient me - rit Raise us to thy glo - - rious
f

172
ff
unis.
throne.
Come, thou long-ex - pect-ed Je - sus,
ffp
unis.
ff
Come,
thou long-ex - pect-ed
ff
175
come, thou long-ex - pect-ed Je - sus,
Come, Lord Je - sus,
Je - sus,
come, thou long-ex - pect - ed Je - sus,
178
fff
rit.
Come, Lord Je - sus, come, Lord Je - sus, come!
fff
rit.
fff

Optional READING: Isaiah 11: 1–4a (or 1–10)

# 8. O Root of Jesse | O Radix Jesse

Great 'O' Antiphon No. 3, paraphrased AB

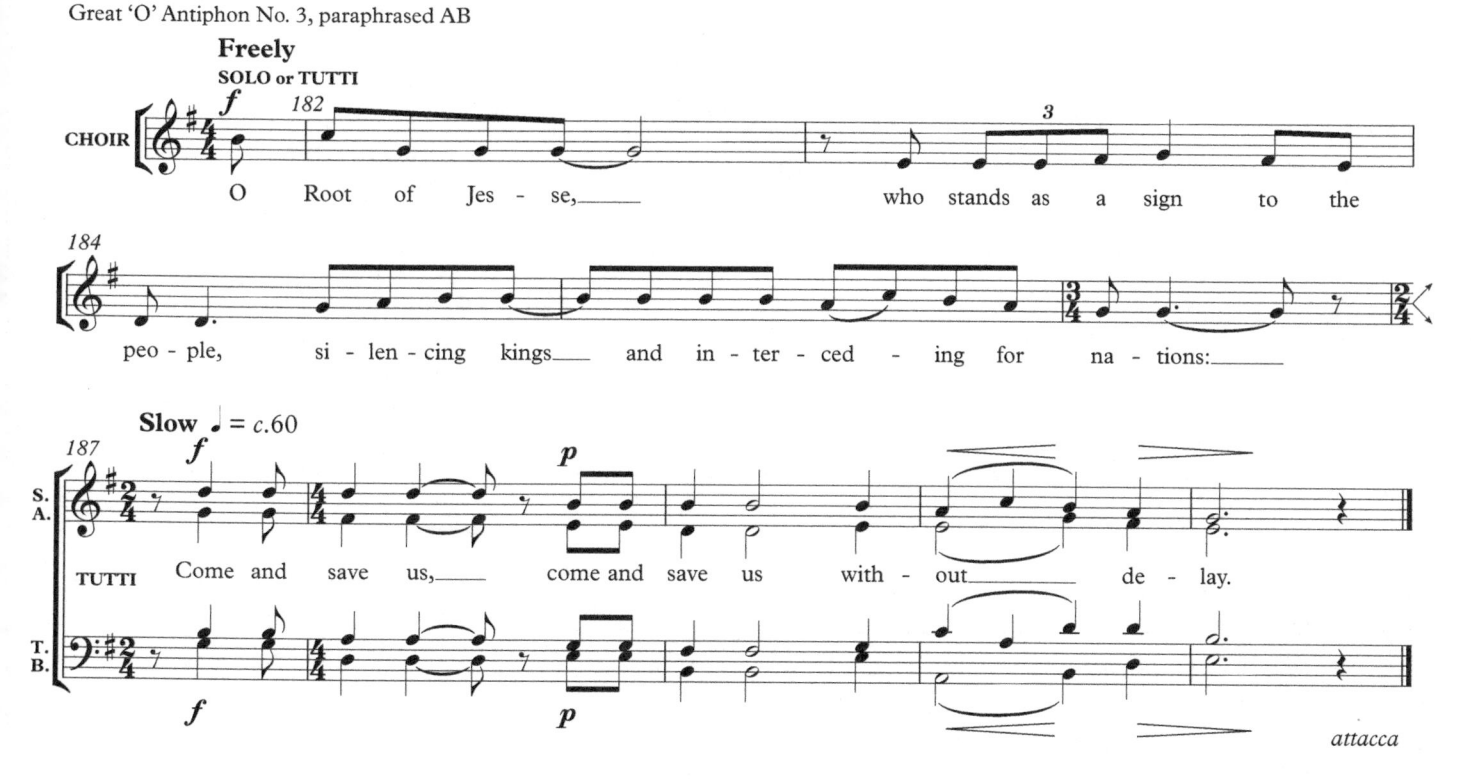


*In grateful memory of my teacher, Herbert Howells*

# 9. Choir: There is a rose-tree

*Es ist ein Ros entsprungen* (German 15th cent.)
translated by Abbie Farwell Brown (1871–1927), altd.

Alan Bullard

201
f
mp
ah
tem - pest can re - move.
2. It was I-saiah who told us: This rose of which we sing
mf
f
206
ah
Brings us the Vir - gin Ma - ry, The mo-ther of our King.
f
It is the Rose of Love, No
f
211
f
pp
cru - el wind can wi - ther, No tem - pest can re - move.
3. Lo, a - ny life that
f
pp
215
mp
p
shiv - ers May shel-ter 'neath that tree,
Each ten-der pe - tal qui - vers With glow-ing mys - te - ry.
mp
p
A little slower ♩ = c.56
p sempre, espress.
rit.
pp
220
A-mid the sweet - ness curled
A gold-en heart is hid-den, The fu - ture of the world!
p sempre, espress.
pp

Optional READING: Isaiah 22: 21–3

# 10. O Key of David | O Clavis David

Great 'O' Antiphon No. 4, paraphrased AB

# 11. Choir: Earth grown old

vv. 1 and 3: Christina Rossetti (1830–94), v. 5: Richard Crashaw (1613–49),
vv. 2, 4, and 6: Isaiah 9: 2,6 paraphrased John Morison (1750–98), altd.

Alan Bullard
based on VENI EMMANUEL, trad. and
DUNDEE (FRENCH), Scottish Psalter 1615

245
TUTTI, unis.
S.
A.
old.
2. The race that long in dark - ness pined Have seen a glo - rious light: The
TENORS and BASSES, unis.
T.
B.
Solo
250
peo - ple dwell in day, who dwelt In death's sur-round-ing night.
(Solo)
255
SOLO, as before
S.
A.
3. When will fire break through her screen? And when will life burst through her mould? Earth, re-born, thy

260
TUTTI
f
p espress. e legato
S.
A.
light is seen: Sil - ver, gold.
4. A Child of Hope to us is born, A Son to us is
T.
B.
p espress. e legato
f
p
266
mf
f
giv'n: The tribes of earth ob - ey his word, Like - wise the hosts of heav'n.
mf
f
p
f
f
Ped.
271
mf
ah
ah
unis.
f
5. Wel - come, all won - ders in one sight! E -
f

* If there are few basses, they should sing the upper part in this verse

# *12. Hymn: Thy kingdom come! on bended knee

F. L. Hosmer (1840–1929)

IRISH
From 'A collection of Hymns and Sacred Poems', Dublin, 1749
vv. 2, 4, and 5 arr. Alan Bullard



* This hymn may be omitted if desired

311
see On earth that king-dom's day. p 2. But the slow watch - es of the night Not less to
souls, Pro - claim the day is near: f 4. The day in whose clear - shin - ing light All wrong shall
v. 2: p or tacet
v. 4: f
320
God be - long; And for the ev - er - last - ing right The si - lent stars are strong.
stand re-vealed, When jus - tice shall be throned in might, And ev - 'ry hurt be healed;
SOPRANO DESCANT
f
329
S.
5. When know - ledge, hand in hand with peace, Shall walk the earth a - broad: The
ALL OTHER VOICES
f
A.
T.
B.
5. When know - ledge, hand in hand with peace, Shall walk the earth a - broad: The
f

Optional READING: Numbers 24: 15–17 (or Job 38: 4–7, or John 1: 19–28)

## 13. O Morning Star | O Oriens

Great 'O' Antiphon No. 5, paraphrased AB

**Fast, with excitement** ♩ = *c.*100

**SOLO or TUTTI**

# 14. Choir: Chanticleer

William Austin (1587–1633)

Alan Bullard

**chanticleer* = a crowing cockerel

365
molto rit.
wake and rise!
molto rit.
369
♩. = ♩ Slower, with mystery
pp
ff
See a won - der Heav'n is un - der;
pp
ff
♩. = ♩ Slower, with mystery
(double choir ad lib.)
pp
Ped.
(Piano: + 8va bassa)
Tempo 1, lively
375
mf
f
mf
From the earth is ris'n a Sun,
Shines all night, shines all night,
Shines, shines all night, shines all
mf
f
mf
Tempo 1, lively
mf
f
Man.

379
f
shines all night, though day be done.
night, all night, though day be done.
f
f
Ped.
Man.
383
unis.
p
mf
Wake, O earth, wake ev - 'ry - thing!
unis.
p
mf
Wake, O earth, wake ev - 'ry - thing!
p
mf
388
f
mf
Wake, and hear the joy I bring:
Wake and joy; for all this night
f
mf
Wake, and hear the joy I bring:
Wake and joy; for all this

393
Heav'n and ev - 'ry twink - - - - ling light,
night Heav'n and ev - 'ry twink - - ling light,
Ped.
397
All a - maz - ing, Still stand gaz - ing.
402
An - gels, Pow-ers and all that be,
Wake and joy, wake and joy,
Wake, wake and joy, wake and
Man.

406
f
wake and joy this Sun to see.
joy, and joy this Sun to see.
f
f
Ped.
Man.
410
f
Hail, O Sun, O bless - ed Light, Sent in - to the
f
mf
f
Ped.
415
rit. molto
mp
world by night! Let thy rays and heav'n - ly pow-ers Shine in these dark souls of ours;
mp
rit. molto
mf
mp
Man.

♩. = ♩ Slower, with mystery and power
420
pp
ppp
ff
For most du - ly Thou art tru - ly God and man, we do con -
pp
ppp
ff
♩. = ♩ Slower, with mystery and power
ppp
p
ff
Ped.
(Piano: + 8va bassa)
Tempo 1, lively
428
ff
- fess: Hail, O Sun, Hail, O Sun,
Tempo 1, lively
ff
ff
432
fff
Hail, O Sun of right - - - - - - eous - ness!
fff
fff

Optional READING: Jeremiah 30: 7–11a (or Jeremiah 10: 6–7, or Isaiah 28: 16–17)

# 15. O King of the Nations | O Rex Gentium

Great 'O' Antiphon No. 6, paraphrased AB

**Lively** ♩ = *c.*100

**TUTTI or SOLO**

# 16. Hymn: Joy to the world!

Paraphrase of Psalm 98 by
Isaac Watts (1674–1748), altd.

ANTIOCH
From *Voce di Melodia*, W. Holford, *c.*1834
arr. Alan Bullard

464
f
na - ture sing.
2. Joy to the world! the Sa-viour reigns; Let all their songs em-
f
f
470
mf
mp
- ploy;
While fields and flocks, rocks, hills and plains
Re - peat the sound-ing joy, re -
Re - peat the sound-ing
mf
mp
mf
mp
474
f
- peat the sound-ing joy, re - peat, re - peat the sound-ing joy.
joy, re - peat the sound-ing joy, re - peat the sound-ing joy.
f
f
f

478
p
mf
3. No more let thorns in - fest the ground, Or sins and sor - rows grow. Wher-
p
mf
3. No more let thorns in-fest the ground, Or sins and sor - rows grow.
p
483
-ev - er trou - bles and cares are found He makes his bless - ings flow, he
Wher-ev - er trou - bles and cares are found He makes his bless - ings
mf
(double voices ad lib.)
486
f
makes his bless-ings flow, he makes, he makes his bless - ings flow.
f
flow, he makes his bless-ings flow, he makes his bless ings flow.
f

490
SOPRANO DESCANT
S.
f
4. He rules the world with truth and grace, And makes the
ALL OTHER VOICES
A.
T.
B.
f
4. He rules the world with truth and grace, And makes the na - tions
494
na - tions prove The glo - ries of his right - eous-ness And won-ders of his love, and
prove The glo - ries of his right - eous - ness And won-ders of his love, and
498
rit.
ff
won-ders of his love, and won - ders, won - ders of his love.
ff
won-ders of his love, and won - ders, won - ders of his love.
rit.
ff

Optional READING: Matthew 1: 18–23

# 17. And they shall call his name Emmanuel

Matthew 1: 23

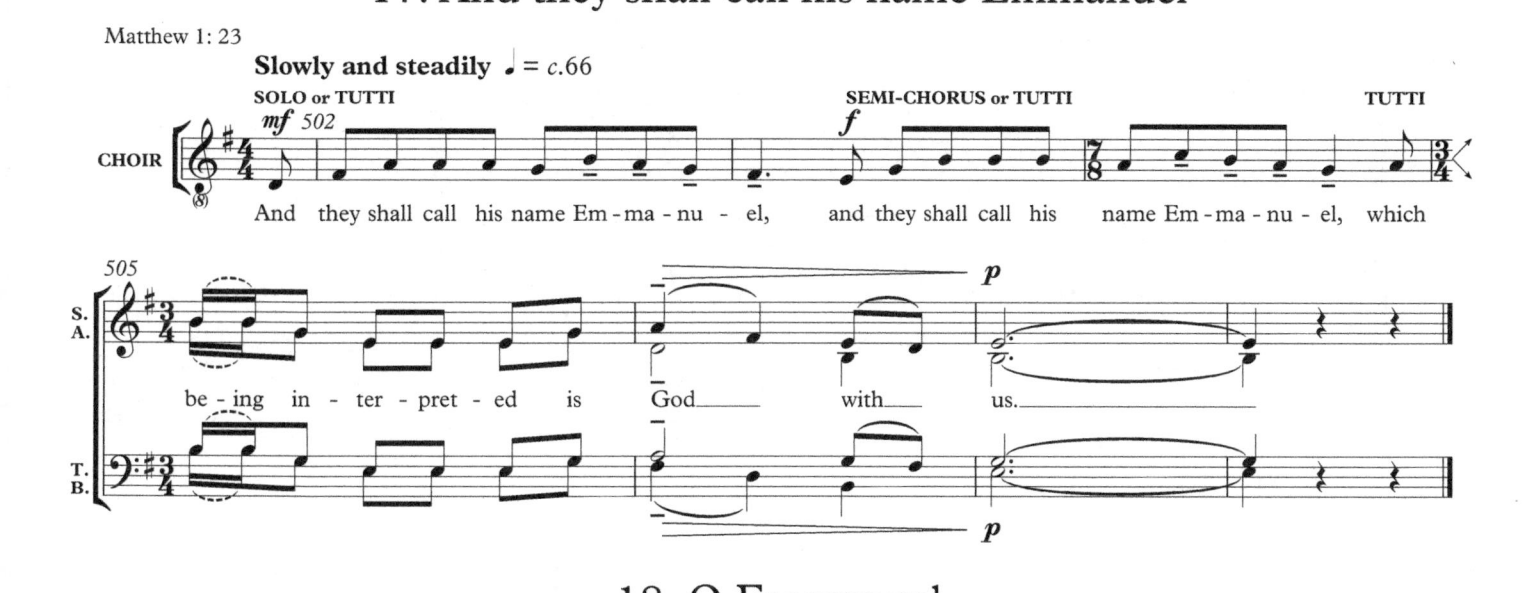


# 18. O Emmanuel

Great 'O' Antiphon No. 7, paraphrased AB

# 19. Choir: Gabriel's Message

Traditional text
paraphrased S. Baring-Gould (1834–1924)

Traditional Basque carol
arr. Alan Bullard

545
S.
A.
T.
B.
p
'For known a bless - ed mo - ther thou shalt be, All
548
hon - our thee,
mf
ge - ne - ra - tions laud and hon - our thee, Thy son shall be Em-ma - nu - el, by
551
seers fore - told.
Most high - ly fa - voured la - dy'. Glo - - - ri-
Most high - ly, most high - ly fa-voured la - dy'. Glo -

554
mf
SOPRANOS and ALTOS unis.
p
-a!
- - ri - a!
Then gen - tle Ma - ry meek - ly
mf
p
558
S.
A.
mf
S.
A.
bowed her head, 'To me be as it pleas - eth God,' she said. 'My
mf
561
Most high - ly fa-voured la - dy.
soul shall laud and mag - ni - fy his ho - ly name':
Most high - ly fa - voured
564
Glo - - - ri - a!
la - dy. Glo - - - - ri - a!

567
S.
A.
T.
B.
f
Of her, Em-ma - nu - el the Christ was born In
570
Christ - mas morn,
Beth - le-hem, all on a Christ - mas morn, And Christ-ian folk through-out the world will
Christ - mas morn, Christ-ian folk
573
p
ev - er say: 'Most high - ly fa - voured la - dy, high - ly fa - voured la - dy'.
ev - er say: 'Most high - ly fa - voured la - dy, high - ly fa - voured la - dy'.
ev - er say: 'Most high - ly fa - voured la - dy, la - dy'. Glo -
mp
ev - er say: 'Most high - ly fa - voured la - dy, high - ly fa - voured

576
mp
mf
Glo - - - - ri - a, glo - - - - ri - a, 'Most
Glo - - - - ri - a, glo - - - - ri - a, 'Most
- - - ri - a, glo - - - - ri - a, 'Most
la - dy'. Glo - - - - ri - a, glo - - - - ri -
rit.
allargando molto
579
f
ff
high - ly fa - voured la - dy.' Glo - - - - ri - a!
high - ly fa - voured la - dy.' Glo - - - - ri - a!
high - ly fa - voured, high - ly fa - voured la - dy.' Glo - ri - a!
- a, 'Most high - ly fa - voured la - dy.' Glo - ri - a!

# 20. Choir: And art thou come with us to dwell?

Dora Greenwell (1821–82) altd.
Latin trad. tr. J. M. Neale (1818–66)

Alan Bullard
based on VENI EMMANUEL
(Anon. 15th century)

* Always phrase and accentuate naturally with the words

598
breaks the rose In tri-umph o'er the griev - ing thorn.
cap - tive Is - - ra - el.
SOPRANO 2 SOLO (or TUTTI SOPRANOS)
603
p
mf
S.
3. Thou bring-est all a - gain; with thee Is light, is space, is breadth, and room
p
mf
607
For each thing fair, be - loved and free, To have its hour of life and bloom.

612
(S 2. SOLO or TUTTI S.)
mp
p
S.
4. Each deep - est in - stinct, un - con - fessed; Each hid - den root, each cloud a - bove,
A. (+S.) unis.
A. (+S.)
That mourns in lone - ly ex - - - ile here,
T. + B. unis.
T. B.
616
mf
And all that life hath long re - pressed, Un - folds, re - veal - ing joy and love.
Un - til the Son of God ap - pear.
622
SOPRANO 1 SOLO (or TUTTI SOPRANOS)
5. Thy reign e - ter - nal will not cease; Thy years are sure and
SOPRANO 2 SOLO (or TUTTI ALTOS)
S. (A.)
5. Thy reign e - ter - nal will not cease; Thy years are sure and glad, and strong,

626
glad, and strong, With-in thy glo-rious world The hum-blest crea-ture makes its song.
With-in thy glo-rious world of peace The hum-blest crea-ture makes its song.
631
SOPRANO 1 and 2 SOLO (or TUTTI SOPRANOS)
S.
f
6. The world is glad for thee: the heart Is glad for thee, and all is well And fixed, and sure, be-cause thou
A. (+S.)
unis.
A. (+S.)
Re - joice, re - joice, Em - ma - nu - el Shall come to thee, O Is -
T. + B.
unis.
T. B.
638
rit. molto
pp
art, Whose name is called Em - ma - nu - el, Em-ma - nu - el.
- ra - el. Em-ma - nu - el.
rit. molto
pp

Optional READING: Revelation 22: 12–13, 16–17, and 20, and/or optional PRAYERS

# 21. Advent Responsory (ii)

The Vesper Responsory

Alan Bullard, based on HELMSLEY
Martin Madan (1726–90)

a tempo
TUTTI or SOLO
657
f
Stand ye still, and ye shall see the sal - va - tion of the Lord.
mf
662
mf
f
S.
A.
Glo - ry, glo - ry
Glo - ry, glo - ry be to the Fa - ther, and
T.
B.
mf
f
f
666
poco rit.
p
to the Son, and to the Ho - - - ly Ghost.
p
poco rit.
p
attacca

# 22. Hymn: Lo! he comes with clouds descending

Charles Wesley (1707–88) altd.

HELMSLEY
Martin Madan (1726–90)
vv. 2–3: harmonisation from English Hymnal
vv. 1 and 4: arr. Alan Bullard

*Verse 3 may be omitted

720
p
mf
Lord, have mer - cy, Lord, have mer - cy, Lord, have mer - cy, Let us
Sing ho - san - na, Sing ho - san - na, Sing ho - san - na, See, the
727
f
1.
2.
all thine Ad - vent see!
ri - sen Lord ap - - pears!
732
SOPRANO DESCANT
S.
4. Yea, A - men! let all a - dore thee, High on
ALL OTHER VOICES
A.
T.
B.
4. Yea, A - men! let all a - dore thee, High on
738
thine e - ter - nal throne; Sa - viour, take the pow'r and glo - ry:
thine e - ter - nal throne; Sa - viour, take the pow'r and glo - ry:

745
mf
Claim the king - dom for thine own: O come quick - ly!
Claim the king - dom for thine own: O come quick - ly!
751
f
ff
allargando
O come quick - ly! O come quick - ly! Al - le - lu - ia!
O come quick - ly! O come quick - ly! Al - le - lu - ia!
757
a tempo
rit.
Come, Lord, come!
Come, Lord, come!
fff